W9-ACS-771

Pudmuddles

by Carol Beach York

pictures by Lisa Thiesing

HarperCollins*Publishers*

Pudmuddles
Text copyright © 1993 by Carol Beach York
Illustrations copyright © 1993 by Lisa Thiesing
For information address HarperCollins
Children's Books, a division of HarperCollins Publishers,
10 East 53rd Street, New York, NY 10022.
1   2   3   4   5   6   7   8   9   10

First Edition

Library of Congress Cataloging-in-Publication Data
York, Carol Beach.
  Pudmuddles / by Carol Beach York ; pictures by
Lisa Thiesing.
      p.   cm.
  Summary: After their marriage, Mr. and Mrs. Pudmuddle
move into their backwards house where they live happily until
they discover certain deficiencies—there is no basement and
the roof has blown off.
  ISBN 0-06-020436-2. — ISBN 0-06-020437-0 (lib. bdg.)
  [1. Dwellings—Fiction.   2. Humorous stories.]
I. Thiesing, Lisa, ill.   II. Title.
PZ7.Y82Pu   1993   91-23596
[Fic]—dc20   CIP
                                              AC

For Diana
—C.B.Y.

For Connie
—L.T.

One

Mr. Pudmuddle always ate his dinner in the morning and his breakfast at night.

He always went on a picnic first and packed his picnic basket afterward. (This fooled the ants.)

He went to the store and then came home and made out his shopping list.

He put on his clothes and then took his bath.

When he had been a small boy, he had eaten wonderful things—soodle noup and tuttered boast and pollilops. He had sat in his kitchen with his cots and pups and prying fan, and eaten as

1

many sam handwiches as he wanted, and nobody had said no.

Even now, when he was grown up, he still liked soodle noup for lunch.

As the years passed, Mr. Pudmuddle dreamed of finding the right person to be Mrs. Pudmuddle. They would share their lives and their dreams, dinner in the morning and breakfast at night.

Two

The person Mr. Pudmuddle fell in love with was plump and good-natured and very fond of Mr. Pudmuddle.

Wedding plans were made at once; a cake was ordered.

"And we will build a beautiful house to live in," Mr. Pudmuddle said. He went straight downtown to take care of this.

It was a bright spring day, and Mr. Pudmuddle's heart was full of joy. He passed the post office and the town library, tipping his hat to people he

knew—and some he didn't, by mistake.

The town was not very large, and it didn't take Mr. Pudmuddle long to get to the center of it, to the offices of Hustle, Bustle, and Rush. This was *the* place to go for whatever you needed. Hustle, Bustle, and Rush could do just about everything there was to do, and they wasted no time about it.

They pulled teeth and cut hair.

They published the daily newspaper.

They ran the bank and gave out the money.

They sold fine furniture and fudge and fence posts.

They handled great cases in courts of law.

And more.

Hustle and Bustle were small and round. They were rather whiskery. Mr. Rush was long and lean. He didn't eat much. "I have no appetite," he always said. An ice-cream cone meant nothing to him. He had never tasted chocolate pie. Every year he grew more thin. Soon he would probably be gone altogether.

There were two junior partners, Hurry and Scurry, but they were hardly ever seen. They were in the back offices answering telephones and writing letters at such a wild speed, you wouldn't believe it even if you saw it with your own eyes.

"I'm going to be married," Mr. Pudmuddle told Hustle, Bustle, and Rush, "and I would like to build a house."

"Yes, yes, build a house . . . we can easily do that."

"I have a nice bit of land by the river," Mr. Pudmuddle said. "I want to build a house there. As fast as possible," he added.

Well, he had certainly come to the right place.

"As fast as possible is our motto." Mr. Bustle pointed to the words AS FAST AS POSSIBLE in a frame on the wall of the very room where they sat.

"I would want a kitchen in the front," Mr. Pudmuddle said, liking things backward. "A cozy kitchen with flowerpots on the windowsills and a cookie jar that is never empty and chairs enough for everybody if company comes."

"Of course, a kitchen," Hustle, Bustle, and Rush agreed at once.

"And a bedroom," Mr. Pudmuddle said.

"Yes, yes."

"A dining room," Mr. Pudmuddle continued.

(Mr. Rush was not sure this was necessary.)

"A living room," Mr. Pudmuddle said, "with a fireplace and a deep carpet and a couch, where you can curl up to read books on rainy days."

"A living room is always nice." Hustle, Bustle, and Rush nodded as one.

"A front porch on the back," Mr. Pudmuddle finished up, "with a swing, and a table for lemonade."

When all this was settled, Mr. Rush himself seized a large book entitled *Handyman—Volume Three: How to Build a House* and hurried off to Mr. Pudmuddle's bit of land by the river.

Close behind Mr. Rush came trucks bearing bricks and boards and brass knobs for the doors.

Close behind the trucks came furniture vans from the FINE FURNITURE, FUDGE, AND FENCE POST store.

By nightfall the house was built and

the furniture was in place. The windowsills had flowerpots, and the cookie jar had cookies. The swing was hung on the front porch and the fireplace was full of wood (for when winter came). Mr. Pudmuddle was able to eat breakfast in his new dining room and go to sleep in his new bedroom. He could hear the river gurgling by in the moonlight, and he was very content.

Three

However, there were a few mistakes.

The bathtub had been put on the wrong side of the bathroom door, which is to say that it was out in the hall.

"Never mind," Mr. Pudmuddle said to himself. "It will be handy to keep books and things in, between baths."

In the kitchen, hot water came out of the COLD faucet and cold water came out of the HOT faucet.

"I rather like that," Mr. Pudmuddle said.

There were three stairways in the house: one in the front so you could go

11

upstairs, and one in the back so you could come down again, and one stairway leading nowhere at all, because it had been built hastily, without thought.

Mr. Pudmuddle didn't mind. He liked the stairway that led nowhere. He could sit there and be peaceful and quiet. Nobody would disturb him, because nobody would be going up or down the stairs.

"Perfectly all right about the stairway," he decided.

Then the house was painted white, the roof was painted red, and everything was done.

The house was finished none too soon. The next day was Mr. Pudmuddle's wedding day.

Hustle, Bustle, and Rush had baked it themselves in a flurry of flour and frosting. It said:

HAPPY BIRTHDAY

"Happy Birthday?" the bride said with surprise when she saw the cake. "Is it your birthday, dear?"

Mr. Pudmuddle looked out the window. No snow was falling, for it was still springtime. "No, it can't be my birthday," he said. "My birthday is in the winter."

"You can have two then," she said. "One in the spring and one in the winter."

"I don't know about that." Mr. Pudmuddle frowned. "Does that mean I would get old twice as fast?"

"I don't think so," said the bride. "It would just mean you would get twice as many presents."

That sounded good to Mr. Pudmuddle.

"All right," he said, "this can be one of my birthdays."

Everybody cheered and sang Happy Birthday to Mr. Pudmuddle. Then they cut the cake and ate it. (Mr. Rush refused a slice because, of course, he had no appetite.)

The bride threw her bouquet first and came down the aisle to get married afterward. Mr. Pudmuddle kissed her once and put the wedding ring on her finger. A perfect fit.

Then the minister married them.

Last of all, the organist played "Here Comes the Bride."

Five

Mrs. Pudmuddle loved the house Mr. Pudmuddle had built for her.

She didn't mind the stairway that went nowhere. Or the kitchen faucet where the hot water came out of the faucet marked COLD. "I can get used to that," she said—wrapping her burned finger.

But she did *not* like the tub in the hall.

When she first saw it, she was still in her wedding dress. She had the heavy train to drag by herself, for the six bridesmaids were gone. She had discovered that her wedding slippers were too tight for comfort. Also, it was warm.

And there in her beautiful new house was a big bathtub in the middle of the hall.

And in the tub were books, two coat hangers, and yesterday's newspaper (published by Hustle, Bustle, and Rush).

"We must move this tub," she said. "The hall is too cold and drafty for a bath."

Mr. Pudmuddle—dressing first, then taking his bath—never minded drafts.

"And I need my privacy," Mrs. Pudmuddle said. "One can't take a bath right in the middle of the hall."

So the tub was moved into the bathroom, where it belonged in the first place.

Then Mrs. Pudmuddle moved in— which was a wonder to behold.

She had seventeen umbrellas and thirty-two teapots. She also collected bells and clocks and silver spoons (drawers and boxes and cupboards full). She collected postcards from people who went traveling and wrote to her about it.

She collected recipes and thimbles and calendars. Mr. Pudmuddle always knew what month it was after Mrs. Pudmuddle moved in with her calendars.

She collected too many things to name them all.

But by and by, everything she had was moved into the new house, the clocks wound up and ticking and chiming and cuckooing twenty-four hours a day.

Mr. Pudmuddle was as proud of all this as if he had collected everything himself.

Six

Mrs. Pudmuddle knew Mr. Pudmuddle ate dinner in the morning and breakfast at night.

On her first night in the new house she hung her apron on the bedpost, so she would be ready to help with the morning dinner.

She woke early, but Mr. Pudmuddle was already up. He was already busy in the kitchen.

Mrs. Pudmuddle tied on her apron and went to help.

The sun was rising.

Flowers were opening.

Dew was sparkling on the grass.

Mr. Pudmuddle was rolling out a piecrust—he always started meals with dessert first.

Mrs. Pudmuddle chopped lettuce and carrots for a salad.

She boiled green beans.

She stuffed a chicken and popped it into the oven.

Pans and bowls and stirring spoons were everywhere.

Mr. Pudmuddle peeled potatoes.

He put the kettle on to boil water for tea.

He put butter in a dish and polished the butter knife.

Mrs. Pudmuddle baked bread.

She put out napkins.

Plates.

Knives and forks and spoons.

Mr. Pudmuddle poured tea into the

water glasses and water into the teacups.

Mrs. Pudmuddle was pretty tired now.

But as the clocks struck eight, dinner was ready.

"This is wonderful," Mr. Pudmuddle said, looking at the laden table.

Mrs. Pudmuddle was so thrilled by this praise that, with her strength revived, she ran out into the garden and gathered a bouquet of lilacs for the dinner table.

Her reward came at sundown, when they only had to fix a simple breakfast of tuttered boast.

 Seven

Everything went along very well for several days. Perhaps it was a whole week.

Then Mrs. Pudmuddle decided to plant a flower garden.

Mr. Pudmuddle got out all the vases. It was his rule: vases first, then the flowers.

When the vases were ready, the Pudmuddles went into town and bought six packages of flower seeds and some garden tools: hoe, rake, trowel, and spade.

And then a terrible discovery was made.

There was no basement in their house.

Hustle, Bustle, and Rush had been so intent on speed, they had forgotten a basement and had begun right away with the house.

The proper place to keep garden tools is in the basement, so you can see there was a problem.

Mr. Pudmuddle got right on the telephone and called Hustle, Bustle, and Rush to complain—although he was very polite about it. He said perhaps, if it wasn't too much trouble, perhaps there should be a basement. . . .

"Handy in the winter, too," he added. "We could put a furnace there and keep the house warm."

Mr. Pudmuddle was not too upset.

To him it seemed quite the ordinary thing to build the house first, then dig the foundation.

Hustle, Bustle, and Rush agreed that a basement was a splendid idea.

(The junior partners, Hurry and Scurry, agreed too, although no one had really asked them.)

Without delay, an enormous truck arrived and hauled the Pudmuddles' house off to the far side of the yard—mashing down the flower-bed dirt rather a lot, which was too bad but couldn't be helped.

Then a basement was dug, to be under the house when the house was brought back from the flower bed.

"This is a mess," Mrs. Pudmuddle remarked. And she was usually so cheerful. You could see it was a strain on her. As the house was brought back, glasses

rattled dangerously in the cupboards, the piano slid across the living room and back again, and other furniture was re-arranged. Mr. Pudmuddle couldn't get into his closet because his bed had gone over against the closet door, and the dining-room table was in the hall where the bathtub had been (good thing it was gone).

Mr. Rush came forward proudly when all was done.

"Now you have your basement," he said.

And that part was good. Now there was a place for the hoe, rake, trowel, and spade; a place for a furnace to keep the house warm in winter; a place to roll up the garden hose when summer was over; and a place to hear strange sounds from on spooky dark nights. Soon a mouse moved in, and then a small spider, and the basement was complete.

The unfortunate part was that Mr. Pudmuddle lost his stairway-that-went-nowhere, his sitting, private place. For now it was discovered that these stairs led down into the basement, and there was coming and going on them all day long.

Mrs. Pudmuddle liked to go down there and put labels on her jelly jars and admire her new washing machine.

She rearranged shelves and polished things that need polishing.

She started a collection of flower pictures cut from the seed catalogues stored with the garden tools.

Mrs. Pudmuddle loved her basement. Mr. Pudmuddle missed his stairway.

However, it was not his nature to be sad for long. He found a tree at the far end of the backyard that was rather private and could be his. He often sat there and thought interesting, noble thoughts—or just daydreamed. By and by, he decided that his tree was even better than his stairway had been.

 Eight

Mrs. Pudmuddle soon grew used to Mr. Pudmuddle's ways.

He played the piano and learned the music afterward.

He read the last page of a book first, to see where the story was going.

He knew the alphabet from ZYX all the way back to CBA.

After his bath his shoes squeaked, but all his clothes were clean.

On Sunday they had their dinner first and then went to church.

They were very happy together—and everything was fine at the new house—until one day the roof blew off.

Summer was ending and the days were getting shorter. Leaves were turning golden on the trees by the river; on Mr. Pudmuddle's tree, too. A strong wind rose up suddenly late one afternoon. And the roof blew right off the house.

The Pudmuddles didn't know their roof had blown off until they saw roof shingles and chimney bricks flying down into their yard. They were just having their evening breakfast—and off came the roof.

"I hope it doesn't rain tonight," Mrs. Pudmuddle said. "Fortunately we have umbrellas." (Seventeen.)

"A useful collection," Mr. Pudmuddle agreed.

They went all over the house and put up umbrellas to keep the furniture dry if it rained.

Mr. Pudmuddle said he had always wanted to sleep under the stars.

For Mrs. Pudmuddle, one night of sleeping under the stars was enough. She was not a gypsy at heart. The very next morning Mr. Pudmuddle went personally to see Hustle, Bustle, and Rush to tell them about his roof.

"Blown off?"

Hustle, Bustle, and Rush were amazed and dashed out to the house to see for themselves. Ah! It was true. The roof was quite gone. Parts and pieces were scattered far and wide. They began at once to prepare a new roof.

Ladders were put in place.

Nails flew everywhere.

Hammers pounded.

There was much shouting of orders.

Chimney bricks arrived in a cart.

Red paint was sent for.

Lids were pried off.

Brushes were plunged in.

Mrs. Pudmuddle watched with some distress.

She remembered the tub in the hallway. The hot and cold faucets. The lack of a basement.

"They go too fast," she whispered to Mr. Pudmuddle.

It was his thought exactly.

Roof shingles flew about.

Chimney bricks crunched into place.

Paint splashed here, there, and everywhere.

Ladders shook.

"Too fast," she whispered again, and amid the commotion, Mr. Pudmuddle called out:

"SLOW DOWN."

No one had ever before said this to Hustle, Bustle, and Rush.

Mr. Rush was painting everything red. Mr. Bustle was pounding nails (also thumbs and fingers). Mr. Hustle was just sprinting off for a new supply of shingles.

"SLOW DOWN."

It was not like Mr. Pudmuddle to shout. But he did. Hustle, Bustle, and Rush looked at each other anxiously.

Slow down? They didn't know if they could do that.

Mr. Rush dipped his brush into the paint can . . . very carefully . . . and painted just a small . . . tiny . . . bit of roof.

Mr. Bustle carefully held each nail and counted to ten before whacking it with his hammer.

Mr. Hustle went up the ladder
one
step
at
a
time
with
the
roof
shingles.
When the new roof was in place it was a good, firm, stay-forever, never-mind-the-wind roof.

Nine

All this was well and good, but it didn't last. Soon Hustle, Bustle, and Rush were back to their old ways—skittering, scattering, scuttling, and scampering to get things done. At breakneck speed they pulled teeth, baked cakes, did this, that, and everything else. By the time they got around to writing the Pudmuddles an apology about the roof, they were again going full speed, and the letter got sent off to the wrong address by mistake:

Mr. and Mrs. Ferdinand Finch
127 Dover Road
Australia

Mr. Finch and his wife were quite surprised to receive this letter.

Dear Sir and Madam,

We are humbly apologetic about occurrences at your house. We are sorry about forgetting the basement and the roof blowing away and the bathtub.

Sincerely Yours,
Hustle, Bustle, and Rush
Cakes for all occasions
Hair cut—Special Rate Tuesdays
Fine furniture, fudge, and fence posts
etc. etc. etc.

As Mr. and Mrs. Finch read the letter, they were greatly puzzled, until they got to the part about Hustle, Bustle, and Rush and the cakes and haircutting.

"Why, this letter isn't for us at all," Mr. Finch said, with some relief. He

had begun to worry about his basement and his roof and his bathtub.

No, of course the letter was not for them. Hustle, Bustle, and Rush had not built the Finch house. The Finch house had been built by Slocum and Poke. Many years it had taken, too. Slocum and Poke's motto was HASTE MAKES WASTE. They didn't get much business, but they hardly noticed, for they were often napping.

Still, Mrs. Finch was curious—about the bathtub part.

"The letter says they are sorry about forgetting the basement and the roof blowing away—*and* the bathtub. Do they mean they forgot the bathtub, or it blew away?"

"Neither is good," said Mr. Finch.

Even though the Pudmuddles never

got this lovely letter of apology, they were very happy in their new home.

The basement was in place.

All the stairways led somewhere.

HOT and COLD water faucets were a small matter (mostly).

The bathtub was on the right side of the bathroom door.

And the roof was on to stay until forever.

By and by, winter came. Snow fell. Mr. Pudmuddle had his wintertime birthday. He blew out the candles first and then made his wish. They watched the snow falling in the woods by the river.

They were always snug and warm in their new house.

They had dinner every morning, breakfast every night, and soodle noup for lunch.

J
FIC
YORK

York, Carol Beach.

Pudmuddles.

526708

DATE			